In memory of the greatest Tennessean I have ever known, my father, Hobert Seth Fleming, Jr.

TENNESSEE

A Bicentennial Celebration

PHOTOGRAPHY AND TEXT BY
JOHN NETHERTON

FOREWORD BY
MARTHA SUNDQUIST

PUBLISHED BY
WESTCLIFFE PUBLISHERS, INC.
ENGLEWOOD, COLORADO

I first discovered John Netherton's photography while staying at a friend's condominium. With a few free hours I looked through his books and came across a beautiful book of pictures from a place called Radnor Lake, a place I had never heard of before. The pictures evoked such a mood of contentment that I was put in mind of Walden Pond, and I resolved that I would someday seek out Radnor Lake.

Little did I know at the time that my husband, Don, would be elected governor of Tennessee, and that we would eventually be living only ten minutes from this tranquil spot. When the rigors of public life and the demands on my time get overwhelming, I now retreat to Radnor Lake for renewal and restoration of spirit.

Nature has always been special in my life and in my husband's. As a young boy growing up, Don spent many happy hours exploring the ravines around his home. He knew where to find the wild ferns, the jack-in-the-pulpits, the spring violets, and the many other wildflowers indigenous to the area.

Don and I are not native Tennesseans but came here as young marrieds with several small children. We first lived in Middle Tennessee—with its gently rolling hills and its wonderful lakes for fishing and boating. We built our first home near Flat Creek on a wooded lot with a backyard full of wild daisies. The children spent much of their time with their friends playing in and around the creek.

After eight years in Middle Tennessee, we moved to Memphis, where in the center of a big city we had to create our own nature preserve by planting trees, flowers, and digging a water lily pond where we could enjoy the dragon flies, the mosquito minnows, the goldfish, and even an occasional raccoon.

As I write this preface in the April of 1995, I am in another borrowed condominium. It sits high above the town of Gatlinburg, and when we arrived the trees were laden with snow and the beauty of the Smoky Mountains was breathtaking. As the day warmed into spring, we could see and hear the snow breaking off the trees and watch the streams grow in size as they rushed down the mountainside. By the next day the daffodils were bright yellow and only the snow in the crevices and shadows reminded us of winter's fast passing.

*Early morning fog clings to fields
of grasses, Cades Cove, Great Smoky
Mountains National Park*

*Preceding Page:
Light filters through fall foliage, Percy
Warner Park*

Tennessee is blessed with a wide variety of terrain and each one has a special place in our hearts, each one brings back special memories. During the campaign for governor, Don and I spent time in many of Tennessee's ninety-five counties, staying as guests in the homes of different people. From one home we could see over into the Cumberland Gap, where the early settlers came into Tennessee. At another we stayed with a young family who raised their own food. We spent a night at a cabin amidst a clearing in the mountains, and in the morning were witness to deer coming to graze. I tried to capture many of these special moments with my camera, but not having an artist's eye, they remain special only to me.

Don and I look forward to visiting many of Tennessee's beautiful parks, places such as the Great Smoky Mountains National Park and the Big South Fork Recreation Area. We want to see the rhododendrons ablaze on Roan Mountain, hike the trails at Fall Creek Falls, cast our fishing lines into the Tennessee River, run the rapids on the Ocoee River, and watch the sunset on the mighty Mississippi. Some of our happiest hours were spent with our children in these activities.

As Tennessee prepares to celebrate its bicentennial in 1996, we become even more aware of how important it is to preserve the natural landscape. We need to introduce our young people to these places so they can learn to appreciate them—and learn the importance of untouched areas in not only the balance of nature but also in maintaining a balance in the human spirit.

As the pictures of Radnor Lake drew me to search it out, I know that this book will lead me to seek many other new places. And I hope John Netherton's photographs will also inspire you to seek out the beauty that is Tennessee.

— Martha Sundquist
First Lady of Tennessee

preface

From my boyhood I have observed leaves, trees, and grass, and I have never found two alike. They may have a general likeness, but on examination I have found that they differ slightly. Plants are of different families....It is the same with animals....It is the same with human beings; there is some place which is best adapted to each. The seeds of the plants are blown about by the wind until they reach the place where they will grow best—and there they take root and grow.

—*Okute, Sioux Indian*

A 19th-century naturalist once wrote in a letter to a friend: "I've been traveling all summer; I got half-way across my backyard." As a native Tennessean, I have been extremely lucky to have this great state as a backyard. After all, how can anyone who earns a living by wandering through mountains engulfed in mist or sloshing through duckweed-covered swamps be considered gainfully employed? Or as my wife, Judy, once put it when asking about a friend: "Does he have a real job, or one like yours?"

I feel that I'm in good company. When John Muir traveled through Tennessee on his thousand-mile journey, he encountered a similar attitude held by a blacksmith who gave him food and lodging for the night.

"Well, young man," the blacksmith queried, "you mean to say that you are not employed by the Government or some private business?"

"No," Muir responded, "I am not employed by anyone except just myself. I love all kinds of plants, and I came down here to these Southern States to get acquainted with as many of them as possible."

"You look like a strong-minded man," the smith replied, "and surely you are able to do something better than wander over the country and look at weeds and blossoms."

My wanderings over the Tennessee countryside have taken me many places to look at weeds and blossoms and all manner of natural things. In Great Smoky Mountains

Water turns to mist at the base of the
main falls, Fall Creek Falls State Park

National Park I have watched hundreds of sunrises and sunsets from atop Clingmans Dome. On hands and knees I have followed salamanders as they traveled to their breeding pools. I've sat quietly on a fallen log in Cades Cove as white-tailed deer walked up to sniff me. I've watched black bears send their cubs scurrying up the tall firs near Mortons Overlook.

Senator Howard Baker, who has a deep love for his home state, first introduced me to Big South Fork. Over the years we have explored the rivers and the impressive canyons they carved over millennia. Poised on the plateau's edge to capture another sunrise on film, I came to understand why a man of his greatness always chose to return to his birth-place of Huntsville, Tennessee.

Rains bring forth hundreds of species of native fungi, Cosby, Great Smoky Mountains National Park

Although my own travels do carry me out of my backyard, I too return home—to my native Nashville. Radnor Lake, for example, continually draws me to its shores, teaching me lessons about nature and about seeing. I remember the first time I photographed Radnor Lake. I approached everything with a cold, scientific manner. While the photographs I took of a killer wasp dragging a cicada to its brooding chamber were technically correct, they did not convey the uniqueness of this place. I would return day after day, only to see a little more each time. The lyrical soon overwhelmed the technical, and the lake was spread out before me in almost a spiritual manner.

I had found my cathedral, my holy grail. For me, this was nature at its best. Like Thoreau's Walden Pond, Radnor Lake became my "tonic of wildness." It is this sense of awe that I have carried with me throughout my more than twenty-five years of photographing the natural world.

The great photographer Ernst Haas once said, "I wanted to be an explorer, and the camera allowed me to be just that." The camera has allowed me to explore too, observing the many wonders of nature. It has allowed me to witness the return of the bald eagle, our national symbol. The bald eagle population, its numbers precariously low, was brought back to self-sustaining levels in Tennessee when managers at Reelfoot Lake and other refuges introduced successful hacking programs. At last count, 246 eaglets have fledged since these programs were initiated.

There are other success stories to be told. Ospreys, which had been reduced to only three nests by 1980, have now recovered and number fifty nesting pairs. The red wolf—virtually hunted to extinction and eliminated in Tennessee—once again roams free in the Smoky Mountains. Even the small boulder darters, a specie that has been the subject of hot environmental debate for years, are now having boulders specially constructed and anchored in the Elk River to provide them a place to deposit their eggs. Of the 125 species of mussels found in Tennessee, 39 are endangered, and refuges are being set aside for their protection.

Tennessee has more federally listed endangered species than any other inland state. Groups such as the Tennessee Ornithological Society have for years worked with federal and local governments to set up habitats for migratory and nesting birds. The Sierra Club, Audubon Society, Tennessee Conservation League, Nature Conservancy, Tennessee Environmental Council, and numerous other organizations have become politically active in protecting Tennessee's environment and indigenous wildlife. Legislation has been passed that allows the establishment of "friends groups" to aid state parks.

Tennessee boasts more than fifty state parks, thirty natural areas, a half dozen national wildlife refuges, the most-visited national park in the United States, and the first national river and recreation area. John Muir walked through what is now Big South Fork; John James Audubon described the earthquake that created Reelfoot Lake; William Bartram wandered the botanical paradise now named the Great Smoky Mountains.

With camera in hand, I too have wandered—sometimes aimlessly, at other times with purpose. As Tennessee now celebrates 200 years of statehood, I give you my vision of the place I call home, and I invite you to join me in exploring the magnificent wilderness I call my backyard.

Eastern bluebird chicks hatch
each spring, Bellevue

Early morning fog separates distant ridges, view from Clingmans Dome, Great Smoky Mountains National Park

mountains

In Tennessee my eyes rested upon the first mountain scenery I ever beheld. I was rising higher than ever before; strange trees were beginning to appear; alpine flowers and shrubs were meeting me at every step. But these Cumberland Mountains were timbered with oak, and were not unlike Wisconsin hills piled upon each other, and the strange plants were like those that were not strange. The sky was changed only a little, and the winds not by a single detectable note. Therefore, neither was Tennessee a strange land.

—*John Muir*

Standing atop Clingmans Dome—at 6,643 feet the highest point in Tennessee—a visitor to the Great Smoky Mountains National Park can watch the sun both rise and set across a sea of layered mountains. On many mornings, these mountains, which are part of the mighty Appalachian chain, are separated by dense blankets of fog that fill the valleys below. Then, all at once, gusts of wind cause the distant ridges to disappear in a misty haze. Visibility is soon limited to just a few yards, and only the mountain ash trees are discernible, their gray limbs covered with brilliant green clusters of lichen and tipped with bright red berries. Juncos flit about on the forest floor, while ravens abandon the tops of majestic fraser firs and fade into the shadowy vapors. At this altitude, clouds blow in and out all day, causing the temperature to drop even in summer and sending park visitors running for the warmth of their car heaters.

Mountains define the eastern edge of Tennessee, gently rising upwards to 6,000 feet. Much older than the Rocky Mountains to the west, the Appalachians have been worn down by time and they are rounded in appearance, cloaked in heavy vegetation. Great Smoky Mountains National Park is the major attraction here. Drawing nearly eleven million visitors a year, it is the most-visited national park in the United States. The United Nations has designated the park as an International Biosphere, one of approximately 300 areas worldwide that has been deemed a unique ecosystem worthy of protection. Indeed, the park and the surrounding mountains are a botanical garden of Eden.

More than 1,500 species of flowering plants are found here, where spring climbs the mountainsides a few feet each day. In late March, bloodroot pushes through the fallen leaves in Cades Cove. By mid-April, the base of the Chimneys is blanketed by what looks like snow from a distance, but which turns out to be the tiny petals of hundreds of thousands of white-fringed phacelia growing amid various kinds of trillium. During July and August, the purple-fringed orchid blooms atop Clingmans Dome. Asters line the road to the top well into September.

Autumn reverses this pattern. October sees leaves dropping first at the high altitudes, as winds rip the orange, yellow, brown and red leaves from their branches. And so downhill it goes, much faster than it came, until the last of the yellow leaves drop from the state's largest poplar, growing along the Albright Trail.

An area so rich in vegetation provides habitats for numerous species of wildlife. The redcheek salamander, one of many variations of Jordan's salamander (Plethodon jordani), occurs nowhere else in the world. Its range straddles the Tennessee-North Carolina border, a region of mountaintops and forests of fraser fir. The moisture blanketing the moss- and fern-covered forest floor at these altitudes makes this an ideal environment for salamanders. Nearly forty species of these amphibians are found in Tennessee—and more than half indigenous to the Great Smoky Mountains.

The endangered red wolf has recently been reintroduced into the Smoky Mountains.

Nearly killed off by hunters, these animals have the distinction of being the first wolves ever released into a national park. Cades Cove was selected as the initial site, an ideal habitat because it is heavily populated by white-tailed deer, an important food source.

One October morning while photographing deer in the Cades Cove area, I was witness to at least a dozen young bucks running straight for me. I tensed with excitement when I thought I was experiencing a red wolf in full pursuit. As it turned out, I had misidentified the animal—it was just a coyote. This similarity between the red wolf and the coyote may prove its undoing, for the coyote is considered by many in rural areas to be a varmint and can be legally shot and trapped.

The reintroduction program has been a success, and the red wolf has already proven to be an important predator in the park. Scientists have documented that the wolves have fed on wild hogs, an unwanted, non-native species that has been damaging the ecosystem of the area for many years. It will be a difficult task to assure the red wolf does not range outside the park, but its protection is vital if this endangered species is to once again become an integral part of this mountain domain.

Of all the wildlife in the park, the black bear is surely the most sought-after by visitors. Sows emerge in early spring with two or three young cubs and wander the mountains in search of food. Once when I was walking the Bud Ogle Nature Trail in the Roaring Fork section of the park, I heard a faint noise that sounded like honeybees swarming. I approached the sound as quietly as possible and saw a female black bear being suckled by her two small cubs, who were producing the strange sound effects. Roaring Fork Motor Nature Trail and the Cades Cove Loop Road offer the most frequent sightings of these large omnivores. When tourists become too plentiful, however, the mother bear will send her cubs up a tree, well out of sight, until the pesky bipeds become bored and leave.

Black bears are found almost exclusively in the mountainous regions of the state (although some bears have recently been introduced on the plateau). Cherokee National Forest in particular harbors a large population of black bears. This 630,000-acre forest, which runs almost the entire length of Tennessee's eastern border, still offers a few pockets of solitude for those who seek it. The more popular areas are generally crowded though, for Cherokee National Forest sees approximately nine million visitors a year, second only to the Smoky Mountains.

Rhododendron in bloom,
Roan Mountain State Park

One of the best locations to experience the annual spectacle of rhododendrons is Roan Mountain State Park, located in the northeast corner of the state near Johnson City. Every year in July, Roan Mountain is covered with the brilliant purple blooms of these showy shrubs. Rhododendrons often grow among fields of windblown grasses on high mountaintops. These areas, known as grassy balds, are also sanctuary to a number of endangered plants that have become tolerant of the strong winds that rake the landscape.

Today when I stand atop Roan Mountain or Clingmans Dome, I think back to the first time I visited these mountains. It was in the eighth grade on a class field trip. While my teachers understood the significance of visiting such awe-inspiring places, it would be a few more years until I truly felt the lure of the mountains of Tennessee. Now it is a regular pilgrimage. Spring and fall always find me somewhere in their shadow.

mountains

Crested dwarf iris growing along
stream banks, Tremont, Great Smoky
Mountains National Park

Opposite:
Grotto Falls after heavy summer
rains, Roaring Fork, Great Smoky
Mountains National Park

Sunset over layered mountains, Clingmans Dome,

Great Smoky Mountains National Park

A red-colored columbine dangles from a cliffside,
Tremont, Great Smoky Mountains National Park

Mountain laurel, common along mountainous hiking trails,
Mount LeConte, Great Smoky Mountains National Park

Preceding Page:
Early morning sun breaks through a dense fog,
Clingmans Dome, Great Smoky Mountains National Park

Rhododendron blossoms among evergreen

needles, Cherokee National Forest

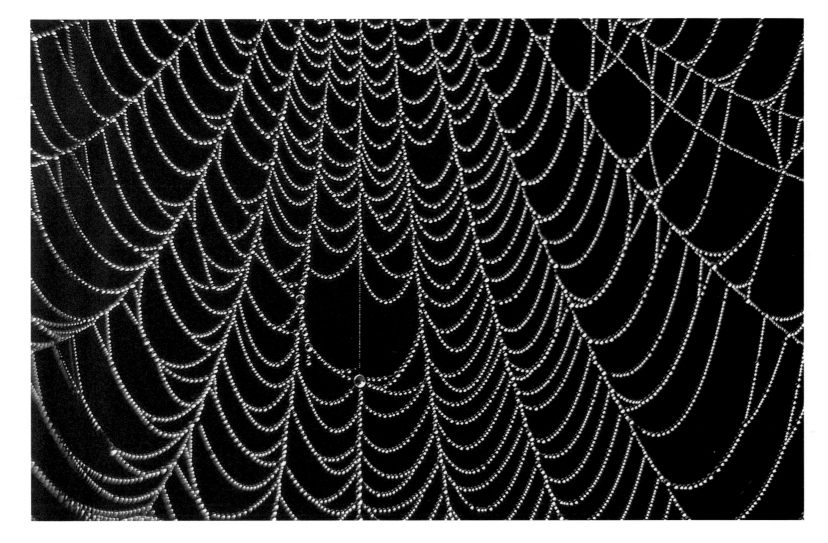

Dewdrops decorate a spiderweb,
Norris Dam State Park

Opposite:
Dogwoods in bloom signal the celebration of the
annual Dogwood Arts Festival, Knoxville

Preceding Page:
A lone deer in Cades Cove,
Great Smoky Mountains National Park

Vivid greens of summer surround a cascading stream,
Roaring Fork, Great Smoky Mountains National Park

*Fields of coneflowers, a sure sign that summer
has reached the mountaintops, Newfound Gap,
Great Smoky Mountains National Park*

A young buck wandering through an open
meadow near the John Cable Mill,
Great Smoky Mountains National Park

Dazzling autumn colors
in the Appalachian Mountains, Newport

The dogwood's fall foliage is just as showy as
its spring blossoms, Johnson City

Opposite:
Ferns rival surrounding trees in autumnal
splendor, Cherokee National Forest

Snow-laden spruce and fir trees atop Newfound Gap,

Great Smoky Mountains National Park

Sunset over Roan Mountain,
Cherokee National Forest

Distant forested mountains stand in contrast to
barren rocky boulders, Cherokee National Forest

Opposite:
Full moon over mountain ridges,
Great Smoky Mountains National Park

Fall colors creep slowly down the mountainsides,
Newfound Gap Road, Great Smoky Mountains National Park

Opposite:
The intense greens of summer surround cascading waters,
Roaring Fork, Great Smoky Mountains National Park

plateau

Goatsbeard blossom veiled by a dew-draped
spiderweb, near Jamestown

Awoke drenched with mountain mist, which made a grand show, as it moved away before the hot sun….Obtained fine views of a wide, open country, and distant flanking ridges and spurs. Crossed a wide cool stream (Emory River), a branch of the Clinch River. There is nothing more eloquent in nature than a mountain stream, and this is the first I ever saw. Its banks are luxuriantly peopled with rare and lovely flowers and overarching trees, making one of Nature's coolest and most hospitable places. Every tree, every flower, every ripple and eddy of this lovely stream seemed solemnly to feel the presence of the great Creator.

—John Muir

John Muir's travels as a young man helped form his ideology, an ideology that would lead to the founding of one of this country's most important conservation groups—the Sierra Club. His thousand-mile journey in 1867 carried him through what is now the Big South Fork National River and Recreation Area. Designated by Congress in 1974, this 106,000-acre area was once the site of lumbering, mining, and oil drilling. Unlike national parks, which generally protect virgin wildernesses, Big South Fork was set aside to allow it to return to its original state. Many of the scars have now healed and much of the area looks as it did more than a hundred years ago when John Muir passed this way.

Big South Fork straddles the Tennessee-Kentucky border on the Cumberland Plateau, a flat, fifty-mile-wide formation that runs parallel to the Appalachian Mountains to the east and rises a thousand feet above the highland rim to the west. It is part of the Appalachian Plateau, a tablelike shelf that stretches along the western edge of the Appalachians Mountains from New York to Alabama. Gorges here plunge hundreds of feet in sheer rock faces, drops in elevation create awesome whitewater rivers.

The New River, the Clear Fork, and the Big South Fork of the Cumberland River offer some of the most challenging rapids for whitewater enthusiasts. Rafting these rivers gives one a sense of being enclosed by massive sandstone walls, rock ramparts carved over hundreds of thousands of years as the rivers flowed through these canyons. The rapids range from Class I, for beginners, all the way to Class VI, for the expert. With names like Devil's Jump and the Washing Machine, these rapids are not for the faint of heart. Angel Falls is so hazardous, in fact, that paddlers are advised to portage around this section.

There are literally thousands of rock shelters on the plateau, and new ones are being discovered all the time. A few years ago I was lucky enough to accompany park archeologist Tom DeJean on one of his many excursions in search of artifacts in Big South Fork. After half a day of swinging from tree limbs over ledges and sliding down steep embankments, we came upon a small waterfall. He explained that many of the falls and rock shelters here are just now being seen for the first time by anyone other than prehistoric visitors and the occasional moonshiner. We named the falls after Senator Howard Baker's late wife, Joy.

Trails have been developed throughout Big South Fork to lead visitors to a number of natural arches and bridges. Twin Arches is an impressive dual span; South Arch extends 135 feet and North Arch measures 93 feet. Arches and chimney rock formations are the park's most popular geological features. Big South Fork is also the site of a recent program by the National Park Service to reintroduce black bears to the plateau. Since lumbering was fairly extensive here before 1974, it will still be a few years before the forest can produce enough mast to support a large population of bear.

Traveling south on the plateau, visitors encounter a number of small parks before reaching one of the more popular state parks—Fall Creek Falls. The main waterfall, for which the park is named, plunges 256 feet into one of the area's many gorges. It is the highest waterfall east of the Rocky Mountains. Cane Creek, Cane Creek Cascades, and Piney Falls are other favorite destinations.

A loop road skirts the edge of the plateau through the park, allowing for magnificent vistas. One of these scenic overlooks, a protruding rock formation called Buzzards Roost, has always been a favorite of mine. Here you can look down at vultures as they ride the air thermals, spiraling slowly upward to eye level, then out of sight. Vultures use small, eroded crevices in the sheer walls for nesting, sites that make it virtually impossible for predators to rob the nests of eggs or chicks.

From Crossville to the Tennessee River, a rift valley splits the plateau. Like many other names in this region, the Sequatchie Valley is of Cherokee derivation. In winter, when trees are bare of leaves, it becomes obvious to drivers on Interstate 24 just how steep and extreme the edge of the plateau is, for it drops more than 1,000 feet to the bottom of the valley. Invariably this section of highway is the first to close to traffic during snow and ice storms. Even when the rest of the state is blessed with sunshine, the top of the Cumberland Plateau may be shrouded in fog.

Along the southern end of the plateau is the 12,000-acre South Cumberland State Recreation Area. Managed as a single park, it is actually seven separate areas, the smallest of which is the Sewanee Natural Area, just two acres in size and featuring a 25-foot sandstone arch. The most noted of the seven is the Savage Gulf State Natural Area, encompassing 11,500 acres. Its magnificent gorges plummet more than 800 feet into virgin wilderness, and scores of waterfalls spray over bright-green mosses and light-colored liverworts. Over fifty miles of trails wind through Savage Gulf, leading visitors among towering trees in stately old-growth forests. Ferns carpet the floor and mushrooms thrive on the moist trunks of fallen trees.

The streams and rivers that lace the plateau eventually drain into valleys that angle toward the Tennessee River. Located north of Chattanooga between the mountains and the plateau, the Ocoee and Hiawassee are popular whitewater rivers. The Hiawassee is the tamer of the two and perhaps the more beautiful, especially the 23.5 miles classified as a National Scenic River. The Blythe Ferry Unit part of the Hiawassee Refuge has become an important stopover for migrating sandhill cranes. While the Ocoee River's flow is regulated by the Tennessee Valley Authority, Class I through Class V rapids can still be experienced at certain points, and the river has been selected as the site for the 1996 Olympic whitewater events.

By all historical accounts, the plateau seems to have been avoided by European settlers and used only sparsely by Native Americans. Its soil is unusually thin, and the sheer drudgery of trying to get on or off the plateau has made it inaccessible to all but the most determined. Even today, travelers on the plateau encounter little development compared to other regions of the state. Yet, in this harshness, nature thrives undisturbed and has created magnificent views of fog-laden forests, sheer canyons, and raging rivers.

The Hiawassee River, 24 miles of which have been classified as a National Scenic River, Cherokee National Forest

Fall Creek Falls, the highest waterfall
east of the Rocky Mountains

Opposite:
Autumn leaves scattered
on a ledge near Ozone Falls

*Yellow lady's slippers, Big South Fork National
River and Recreation Area*

*Preceding Page:
View from the East Rim, Big South Fork National
River and Recreation Area*

Celandine poppies grow on moist hillsides, near Huntsville

Stair-step cascades of Pine Creek, Big South Fork

National River and Recreation Area

Sandhill cranes in flight, near Chattanooga

A tufted titmouse, one of many songbirds that nests in wooded areas, Big South Fork National River and Recreation Area

Trillium, one of the hundreds of wildflowers that
grow in forests on the plateau, Pickett State Park

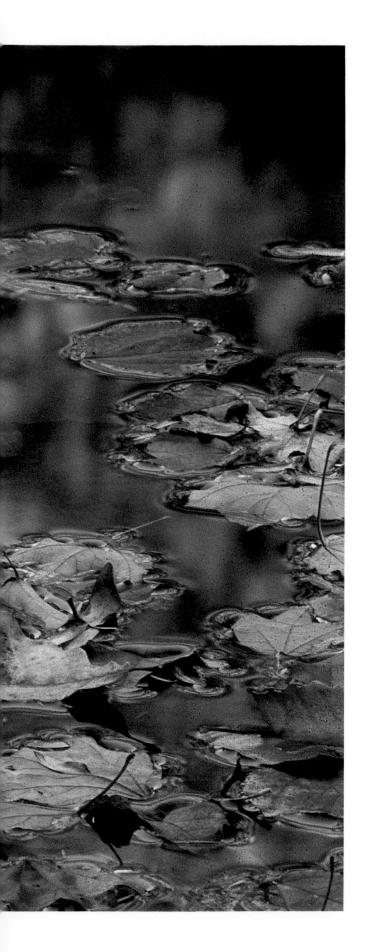

Fall colors reflected in a small pond, near Monteagle

Opposite:
Autumn leaves blanket a pool
of water near McMinnville

White-tailed deer amid fields near Bandy Creek,
Big South Fork National River and Recreation Area

Shafts of light illuminate the woodlands near Spencer

Full moon setting on the Cumberland
Plateau, near Oneida

Buzzard's Roost rises high above the deep
gorges of Fall Creek Falls State Park

*Abstract patterns in sandstone, created by wind
and water, Big South Fork National River
and Recreation Area*

A single maple leaf atop a pine cone, Kingsport

Expansive view of the Cumberland Plateau,

Charit Creek Overlook

Small trickles of water dance down fern-covered ledges,
Rock Island State Park

highland

rim

The Duck and Elk River country was just beginning to settle, and I determined to try that....We got on well enough, and arrived safely in Lincoln County, on the head of the Mulberry fork of Elk River. I found this a very rich country, and so new, that game, of different sorts was very plenty.

—*Davy Crockett*

Tennessee's highland rim is a vast, elevated area that encircles the more populated central basin, rising up about 300 feet above it. The eastern and western portions of the rim are very different in character. The eastern rim butts against the Cumberland Plateau, which rises another thousand feet before leveling off to a relatively flat landscape notched by rivers and streams. This side of the rim could rightfully be called a "land of the waterfalls" due to the sheer number of falls found here. Burgess Falls State Natural Area, perched atop the eastern edge of the rim, is probably the best known.

The Falling Water River is the source of Burgess Falls, which begins its cascade over a few rock ledges just two to six feet in height. The riverbed flattens out for a short distance, then angles down fifty feet into a large canyon. I stopped here on my first visit in the late 1960s, assuming that this section was the main falls. It was years before I went back and finally photographed the 130-foot drop of Burgess Falls. There is a magnificent view of the falls from an overlook built by the state park service, but I am always drawn to the trail that winds through the spray of cascading water and leads to its base. This mist creates an ideal habitat for a luxuriant garden of plants that have adapted to the constant misting and winds created by the falls.

The Caney Fork River sits at the base of the highland rim, supplying Rock Island State Rustic Park with water for a series of falls. My children have taken great pleasure in counting how many times this river disappears beneath a short section of Interstate 40. A trail leads to the limestone riverbed, where boulders, some as large as small cabins, are scattered about. Small spouts of spray drench visitors as they make their way along the base of the cliffs. Footing can be treacherous, as algae-covered rocks create a slippery surface, and the riverbed is spiked with sharp-edged protrusions. A large concentration of vultures, sometimes numbering in the hundreds, can be seen riding the thermals here. In the early morning, before taking flight, these scavengers spread their large black wings to absorb heat from the sun, standing out sharply against the gray rocks.

There is a small cave in the rim's wall where the main waterfall cascades into the river. It is most likely a roost for the thousands of bats that inhabitat the area. Just south of Rock Island, near McMinnville, is Cumberland Caverns, second in miles of passageways only to Kentucky's Mammoth Cave. This area is full of caves and sinkholes.

Traveling a little farther southwest, one runs into the Duck and Little Duck Rivers, which eventually flow into Tennessee's central basin. Waterfalls abound in this area, many of them located on private property. Near Manchester, the Old Stone Fort stands atop the bluffs between two forks of the Duck River. Experts believe that this walled structure dates back to at least A.D. 200. They speculate that it was built by an early agricultural people; more than that is unknown.

The western highland rim is much larger in size than the eastern rim, 7,500 square miles versus 2,500, and it does not boast as many waterfalls. The landscape is characterized by rolling, forested hills, ending near the Tennessee River. The new Natchez Trace Parkway, which follows the original pathway created first by animals, then by Native Americans and European settlers, is one of the most recent areas to be set aside by the National Park Service. There is much history along the Trace: Andrew Jackson marched along it on his way to the Battle of New Orleans; Meriwether Lewis settled here after his cross-country expedition with William Clark in 1804-06; and Davy Crockett likely crisscrossed the Trace many times on his infamous (and numerous) bear hunts.

Beginning near Nashville, the Trace Parkway winds through more than eighty miles of Tennessee countryside and then another 300 miles through Alabama and Mississippi, where it ends in Natchez. White-tailed deer wander the open grassy areas, especially in early morning and late evening. Small flocks of wild turkeys roam the hardwood forests. Several waterfalls—Fall Hollow and Jackson Falls—are but a short walk from the road.

Northwest of Nashville, near Dover, is Cross Creek's Wildlife Refuge. Originally set aside for waterfowl, the 8,862-acre preserve is also an important habitat for migrating and nesting songbirds. Shorebirds also use this area as a stopover, especially when the mudflats are exposed. For several years, the numbers of waterfowl here had declined because so many prairie potholes in the midwestern United States and Canada began drying up. This had the effect of altering migratory routes, as did a serious loss of habitat on private lands as many wetlands were filled in for agricultural use. Through the North American Waterfowl Management Plan, the United States and Canada are now working together with refuges and private landholders to create new habitat.

Downy feather is trapped by lichens and mosses, near Tullahoma

The result has been a marked population increase at Cross Creek, with approximately 93,000 ducks and 73,000 geese each year. The average at any one day during the winter is 20,000 to 30,000 birds, including redheads, common mergansers, pintails, American widgeons, wood ducks, Canada geese, and small numbers of snow and Brandt's geese. At least 276 different species of birds have been identified at the refuge. There are two active bald eagle nests here, and refuge managers have recorded 35 eaglets that have successfully fledged.

The western portion of the highland rim is dissected by three major rivers—the Cumberland, the Buffalo, and the Duck. Near the Duck River is the 5,000-acre Monsanto complex. Monsanto, an example of a corporation working with citizens and government to protect the environment, has set aside 200 acres of ponds to provide habitat for waterfowl and long-legged wading birds.

Today the highland is veined with roads and highways, peopled with towns and cities. Yet in many areas its finger-like cliffs, rolling woodlands, and cascading waters create an image of a landscape little changed during the past 200 years.

highland rim

Water cascading over the upper falls,
Burgess Falls State Natural Area

Opposite:
Redbud trees frame the main falls in early spring,
Burgess Falls State Natural Area

A young opossum hangs from a tree branch, near Columbia

The kingfisher, commonly found near streams and rivers,
announces its presence with a loud chatter, near Tullahoma

Rutledge Falls, one of many waterfalls draining
off the Highland Rim, near Manchester

*Tiger swallowtail butterfly sipping moisture from
decaying leaves, Montgomery Bell State Park*

Spotted salamander heading for a breeding pond
in late winter, Clarksville

Fallen leaf against a lichen-covered rock,
near Smithville

Opposite:
Large boulders near the Buffalo River,
Metal Ford, Natchez Trace Parkway

Dense fog enshrouds lichen-covered trees,
Piney Falls Natural Area

Over time, falling water smooths sharp ledges,
Rock Island State Park

Full moon and fall colors reflected in Radnor Lake,
Radnor Lake State Natural Area, Nashville

central

basin

A lake is the landscape's most beautiful and expressive feature. It is the earth's eye; looking into which the beholder measures the depth of his own nature.

—*Henry David Thoreau*

A female dragonfly glides quietly over the lake's surface, creating ripples as she swoops downward to deposit her eggs in the water. Slowly, the tiny spheres sink into the vegetation at the bottom of the lake. The dragonfly's flight is erratic, zigging and zagging, boomeranging back and forth as she dips the tip of her abdomen just beneath the surface. The water erupts into a spray, much like a small geyser. A large-mouth bass, hiding in the reflection of the water's surface, anticipates the winged creature's next move, and, with no more than a flop back into the water, the fish and dragonfly disappear, leaving only ripples. By the end of their journey, lapping onto the algae-covered shoreline, the ripples have become smooth and leave hardly a trace. This scenario is played out hundreds of times a day at Radnor Lake Natural Area, just outside Nashville.

Nashville is situated on the northwestern border of Tennessee's central basin, a large area in the middle of the state that looks from the air as if it has been scooped out of the neighboring landscape. Long fingerlike ridges border the basin to the east and west, sometimes making it hard to know whether you've entered the highland rim. Surrounded by hills—which are, in turn, surrounded by development—Radnor Lake is one of Nashville's most important green spaces.

A mere seven miles away, the downtown skyline can be seen from Ganier Ridge, the easternmost edge of this 1,050-acre refuge. Created by the L&N Railroad in 1914, Radnor Lake has evolved into a sanctuary for a wide variety of plants and wildlife. The 85-acre lake not only provides habitat for migrating waterfowl, resident muskrat and mink, hundreds of turtles and snakes, and thousands of frogs, but it is also the only state-owned lake of this size mandated to protect its fish species. Nowhere else in Tennessee can biologists observe the behavior and effects of an undisturbed aquatic ecosystem.

My earliest introduction to Radnor Lake came during a highly publicized effort in 1973 to save the area from becoming a residential development. With less than a month to raise a half million dollars (the state and federal governments had already earmarked $3 million for preservation), citizens and environmental groups sold T-shirts and bumper-stickers, held bake sales, and put on any conceivable event they could think of to raise the money. Preserving Radnor Lake was a major victory for the community. For me personally, the lake became my teacher, for this is where I learned to photograph. At Radnor Lake I discovered the writings of Henry David Thoreau, when Dennis Gibson, a long-time Radnor supporter and a good friend, pointed out the similarities between Radnor and Walden Pond. Years later, my photographs were put together in my first book, *Radnor Lake: Nashville's Walden.*

Four miles to the northwest of Radnor Lake is another magnificent sanctuary, Percy and Edwin Warner Park, where 2,681 acres of woodlands and fields are home to deer, fox, woodchucks, and its most famous resident—the Eastern bluebird. Not many years ago, these bluebirds were in serious decline, so an aggressive campaign was launched to put up nesting boxes in Warner Park and throughout central Tennessee. I put up my first bluebird house some six years ago, and since then I have observed and photographed more than fifty young bluebirds as they fledged at these nest sites.

During my youth, Percy and Edwin Warner Park (some people consider it two parks, for it is cut in half by a road) was better known for its recreational facilities—playgrounds, picnic shelters, ball fields, golf and steeplechase courses. Although these activities are still prevalent in the park, there are now sections closed to motorized vehicles, thus preserving large areas of the park strictly for wildlife and its observation. Owl prowls are a favorite activity at both Warner Park and Radnor Lake, and, with a little patience, barred owls can be seen at almost any time of the year—especially when park naturalists lure the birds by imitating their call. I have seen as many as six barred owls come within fifty feet of people and raise enough racket to cause wary children to cling tightly to their parents.

Millions of years ago the area surrounding Nashville actually lay deep beneath the ocean. In one of the oldest fossil rock quarries in the Southeast, located in the community of Una, fossilized coral can still be found in great abundance. The ancient remains of trilobites and brachiopods are evident in quarries close to the Harpeth River, southwest of Nashville.

The Harpeth River first emerges from subterranean beginnings in a very unimpressive ditch. After a great deal of meandering, the river eventually becomes one of the prettiest in all of central Tennessee. It is never so wide that you can't skip a stone across it. It is rarely treacherous, although heavy rains can spill dangerously over its banks. The Harpeth is protected under the National Scenic Rivers Act in Davidson and Cheatham Counties, but, unfortunately, not in Williamson County. While the waters still run clear in this unprotected portion, which is underlain with bedrock and gravel, farther north the river bottom changes and the river runs slower, turning green from algae and sometimes brown from run-off from the surrounding watershed.

Many individuals have made a big difference in maintaining and protecting areas within this region. Basin Springs, for example, a 600-acre refuge near the Harpeth River, was established by Katherine Goodpasture, a long-time conservationist and

Yellow maple leaf against
decaying leaves of the forest floor,
Belle Meade

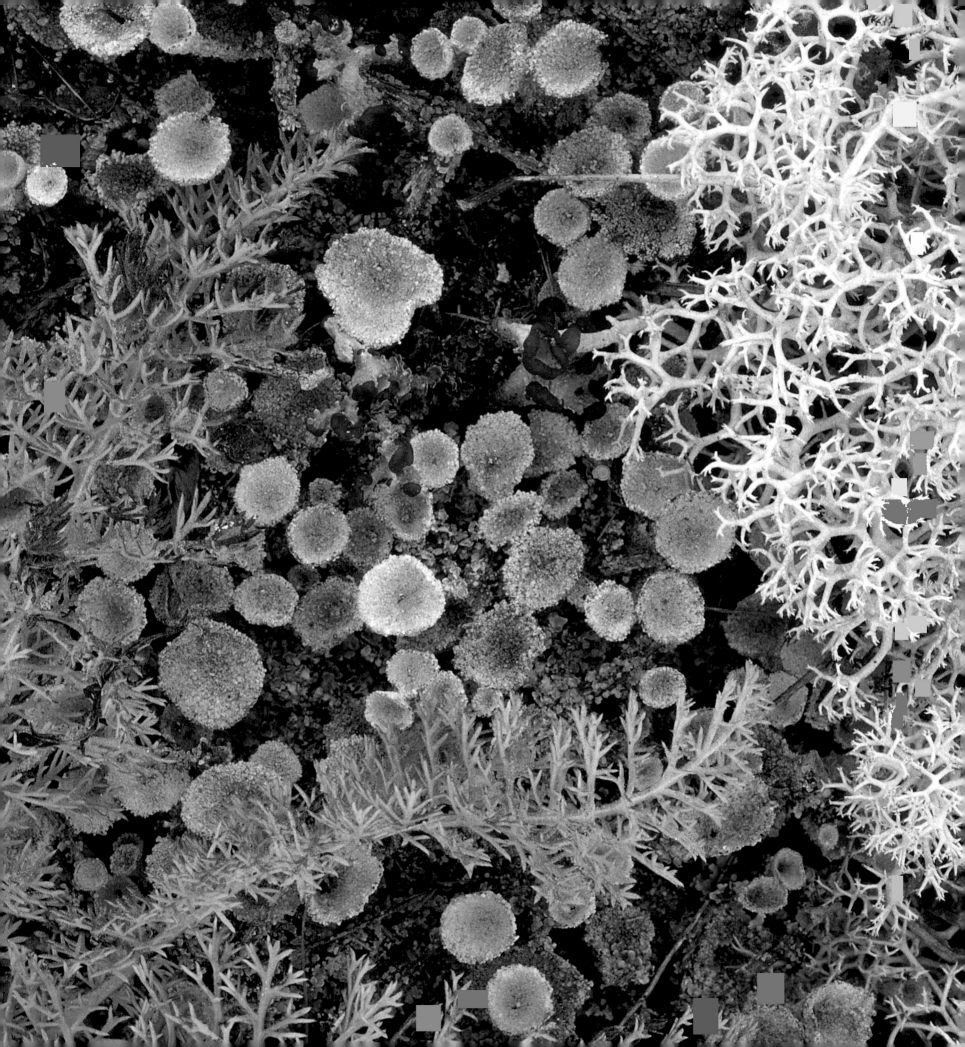

member of the Tennessee Ornithological Society. Millions of birds require habitats such as Basin Springs as a stopover when migrating to and from their South and Central American wintering grounds. Warblers, flycatchers, and vireos are a few of the many species now in serious decline, with habitat loss apparently a major factor. Groups like the Tennessee Ornithological Society are working with the nongame and endangered species programs of the Tennessee Wildlife Resources Agency, as well as with other state and private groups, to create protected corridors for these small birds.

Just east of Nashville, cedar glades dominate the landscape. Twenty-five years ago, these scrubby areas were considered by many to be overgrown trash dumps; today they are protected by federal and state law, and some observers feel this unique ecosystem is the area's most distinguished feature. The glades sit atop limestone bedrock, which supports rare species of plant life, such as the Tennessee coneflower, limestone fame flower, and Gattinger's prairie clover. Lichen and moss carpet the forest floor, while the open areas are more likely to play host to prickly pear cactus and endemic glades flowers.

Numerous sinkholes, surrounded by eastern junipers, leach down into limestone caverns. These caverns are found throughout the entire region, some connecting into more famous caves, like Mammoth Cave National Park in Kentucky. The Nature Conservancy has placed a number of caves under its protection, due to the presence of several species of endangered and rare animals, including the gray and the Indiana bat. Also found here are cave salamanders, crayfish, and blind fish, which survive in complete darkness.

Many years ago the central basin inspired me to pick up a camera and record the wooded, rolling hillsides of this landscape, its tranquil lakes, spectacular spring wildflowers, and colorful autumn leaves. Having lived in Tennessee all my life, I have come to appreciate the state's geographic diversity, with the mountain summits to the east and the flat river valley to the west. It is the central basin, however, that I call home.

*Gray tree frog clings to a
flower stem, Newsom's Station*

*Opposite:
Lichens litter the forest floor
beneath Eastern junipers,
Cedars of Lebanon State Park*

Lone cormorant in the still waters
of early morning, Harpeth River

Autumn leaves cling to a wet ledge,
Richland Creek

Opposite:
Summer storm
over the Cumberland River, Ashland City

First frost, Newsom's Station

Barren limbs form a stark contrast to a
winter sky, Lea's Summit

The state wildflower, the passion-
flower, grows along fence lines
throughout Middle Tennessee

Opposite:
Sunset reflects in placid waters,
Radnor Lake State Natural Area

Abstract ice patterns in a small slough,
Radnor Lake State Natural Area

Snow transforms trees into a winter wonderland,

near the polo fields, Edwin Warner Park

Percy Warner Park, one of
Nashville's premier parks

Abstract colors of autumn leaves,
Marrow Bone Lake

An Eastern bluebird feeding its young through a
hole in a hollowed-out tree, Edwin Warner Park

The haunting trill of screech owls can be heard

in the early evening, Ganier Ridge,

Radnor Lake State Natural Area

Steeplechase fields covered with heavy dew on
a September morning, Percy Warner Park

Bright greens of spring, Deep Well,

Percy Warner Park

Baby cottontails hiding in the grass, their mother
watching from nearby, Indian Springs

Vine-draped trees seen along
roadsides, Brentwood

Field grasses lit by early light, Franklin

Sunrise over misty water,
Radnor Lake State Natural Area

Cypress stand stark against a clear winter sky,
Reelfoot Lake State Park

wetlands

I was [riding] on one afternoon, when I remarked a sudden and strange darkness rising from the western horizon. Accustomed to our heavy storms of thunder and rain, I took no more notice of it, as I thought the speed of my horse might enable me to get under shelter of the roof of an acquaintance, who lived not far distant.... I had proceeded about a mile, when I heard what I imagined to be the distant rumbling of a violent tornado, on which I spurred my steed… but it would not do, the animal knew better than I what was forthcoming, and instead of going faster, so nearly stopped that I remarked he placed one foot after another on the ground, with as much precaution as if walking on a smooth sheet of ice. I thought he had suddenly foundered, and, speaking to him, was on the point of dismounting and leading him, when he all of a sudden fell a-groaning piteously, hung his head, spread out his four legs, as if to save himself from falling, and stood stock still, continuing to groan. I thought my horse was about to die, and would have sprung from his back had a minute more elapsed, but at that instant all the shrubs and trees began to move from their very roots, the ground rose and fell in successive furrows, like the ruffled waters of a lake, and I became bewildered in my ideas, as I too plainly discovered that all this awful commotion in nature was the result of an earthquake.

—John James Audubon

The Madrid Earthquake of 1811-12 was so powerful that it caused the Mississippi River to flow backwards. It also formed many of the wetlands that now dominate West Tennessee. Here slow-moving waters become almost stagnant on the broad flat river plains, creating wetlands that host hundreds of thousands of migrating ducks, waterfowl, raptors, and songbirds.

Reelfoot Lake, located in northwest Tennessee along the eastern banks of the Mississippi River, is a wintering stopover for over a half million ducks and geese. Lesser and greater Canada geese make up ninety percent of the lake's goose population. Snow and blue geese also migrate through on their way to refuges in Louisiana and Texas. Mallards are the most common ducks, along with canvas backs, ringnecks, pintails, wood ducks, and blue- and green-winged teals. At 13,000 acres, Reelfoot is Tennessee's largest natural lake, sometimes expanding to 18,000 acres during winter flooding. Winter also brings a human migration to Reelfoot, as thousands of tourists descend upon the lake from mid-December through early March to watch the bald eagles. Approximately 200 eagles arrive each winter, fishing and scavenging in the cypress-lined waters.

wetlands

In spring and summer amphibians and reptiles dominate the dark waters, some 75 different species in all. Frogs vocalizing throughout the night can at times be almost deafening. Green treefrogs, as well as chorus, leopard, cricket, and bullfrogs—all in search of a mate—churn the shallow waters near the edge of the banks. During the day, stinkpots and sliders sun themselves on half-submerged logs, while eight different species of water snakes glide past lily pads and water lotus blossoms. Visitors often assume that any snake in the water is the notorious cottonmouth. While this snake is a resident, it appears in relatively small numbers, especially since the flooding of 1989. The cottonmouth dens on Reelfoot's islands were flooded that winter, and the snakes suffered great casualties. For this reason, and because of the snake's small-sized clutches of young, it is possible to visit the lake and never see a single cottonmouth.

Reelfoot Lake was formed by the Mississippi River, and one day it will ultimately be erased by the river as well. Silt from the river settles in the wetlands, gradually filling them in. This natural succession—from lake to wetlands and swamp—has been speeded up by the accumulation of agriculture run-off and also by a levee built by the Army Corps of Engineers that prevents the Mississippi from flooding the lake and flushing it out.

In the early seventies, bald eagles were re-introduced to Tennessee, and Reelfoot Lake was one of the principal areas where eagles were released. Reelfoot now has five successful nesting pairs; Land Between the Lakes, owned by the Tennessee Valley Authority, counts seven nests. The hacking program has been so successful that experts in Tennessee's non-game and endangered species program have concluded the bald eagle is now at a self-sustaining level. The osprey has also seen a remarkable recovery in Tennessee's wetlands; in 1980 there were only three active osprey nests in the state and today there are more than fifty.

Wetlands are prevalent throughout West Tennessee, and spring and summer find egret and heron nests crowning the tops of bald cypress trees in Hatchie National Wildlife Refuge, located about an hour east of Memphis near Brownsville. More than 200 species of birds inhabit the 12,000-acre reserve. The elusive river otter is also found here in great numbers.

At Big Cypress Tree State Natural Area, the largest cypress is now only a water-filled stump, having been struck by lightning. Even so, a person in a small canoe can paddle in and turn around in this once-magnificent tree. A small boat is the best way to appreciate the flooded bottomland forests of West Tennessee. From this vantage one can watch wading birds flying in and out of their nesting areas in search of food for demanding chicks. The waters beneath these heronries are gray with excrement, and the odor is enough to keep away all but the most aggressive predators. Great egrets spread their aigrettes—showy trains of feathers—to attract a prospective mate to the nest site the pair will occupy for two months. Loud squawking can be heard as a great blue heron steals a twig from the nest of a snowy egret.

Green tree frog vocalizing,
Obion River

Big Hill Pond State Rustic Park, south of Jackson near the Mississippi border, is not at all what one envisions a wetland should look like. Surrounded by hills, the bottom-land consists of water-tolerant oak, cypress, cottonwood, sweetgum, and tupelo trees. The hills here rise only about 200 feet, but for this area of the state they look almost like mountains. A half-mile boardwalk traverses Dismal Swamp, which, like most of West Tennessee, is only under water during winter and early spring. A 73-foot tower wrapped in chicken wire affords visitors a dramatic view over the miles of forest canopy. Polistes wasps and ladybird beetles swarm atop the tower. When one lands in my hair, I let it find its own way out, not knowing whether it's a beetle, a harmless male wasp, or a not-so-harmless female. Below, I can hear several deer as they walk down to the marshy water's edge.

Standing on a levee on the eastern bank of the Mississippi River, a visitor may feel as though he or she is looking across an ocean; only the silt from the muddy brown waters gives evidence to a river. The sheer massiveness of the Mississippi forces the visitor to marvel why it hasn't cut a straight course to the Gulf of Mexico. Seen from the air, it takes on more of the proportion one feels a river should, as it twines rib-bonlike along the western border of Tennessee. In the northwestern section of the state, the river is normally about a half mile wide. During flood stage however, the river may expand to as much as a mile. Just how much land has been swept away as the mighty river overflows its banks and alters its path again and again is a question that many engineers have pondered.

The eastern boundary of the wetlands is marked by the Tennessee River. An 80-mile stretch in the northern part of the state is the Tennessee National Wildlife Refuge. Divided into three sections—Big Sandy, Duck River, and Bussel Town—the refuge consists of more than 50,000 acres of water, farmland, and woodland. Considered part of the Mississippi flyway, the area is host to more than 150,000 ducks (23 species in all) and 75,000 Canada geese in winter. In summer, osprey and bald eagles nest here, along with egrets, herons, and numerous migratory songbirds.

West Tennessee is not generally considered a big draw for those with a passing interest in wildlife. Its secrets are told to those willing to explore the area chest-deep in waders among the flooded bottomlands or by those willing to portage through muck until a slow-moving stream can float a canoe. There is great beauty in a swamp lit by the full moon, its silvery light reflecting off still waters as barred owls announce their presence with maniacal laughter.

Silhouettes of bald cypress trees,
Reelfoot Lake State Park

Opposite:
Blue heron,
Reelfoot Lake State Park

A water snake, common in the dark, swampy

waters of the wetlands, Brownsville

*Hundreds of turtles, like this small softshell, are found
in many West Tennessee lakes, near Dyersburg*

Anhinga, a frequent summer visitor
to Reelfoot Lake, Blue Bank

Tranquil morning, Natchez Trace State Park

*Lone fisherman slices through the
morning fog, Reelfoot Lake State Park*

Setting sun behind the branches of
cypress trees, Reelfoot Lake State Park

Lilly pads blanket the lake in summer,
Reelfoot Lake State Park

Green tree frog clings to the bottom of a leaf,

near Memphis

The bald eagle, a winter resident of the
Mississippi River and Reelfoot Lake

Calm waters of a summer morn, near Samburg,
Reelfoot Lake State Park

A white squirrel scurries along a
tree branch, Kenton

Opposite:
A great egret stands motionless, waiting for its prey
to come within striking distance, Lower Hatchie
National Wildlife Refuge

Following Page:
Bald cypress trees, nesting sites for numerous
wading birds, Reelfoot Lake State Park

International Standard Book Number: 1-56579-126-6
Library of Congress Card Catalog Number: 95-60671

Photography and text © 1995 John Netherton.
All rights reserved.
Editor: Suzanne Venino
Designer: Nancy Rice, Nancy Rice Graphic Design

Published by Westcliffe Publishers, Inc.
2650 South Zuni Street
Englewood, Colorado 80110

Printed in Hong Kong by C&C Offset Printing

Images from this book are available as 16x20 EverColor DyePrints through Moments in Time Limited.

Each print is registry numbered and issued with a certificate of authenticity signed by the artist and EverColor's master printer, William Nordstrom. Single prints, exhibit matted and ready to frame, are $295. See pages 34-35, 44-45, 46, 96, 105, and 106-107 for photographs available through this special offer.

TO ORDER, CALL 800-533-5050 TOLL-FREE